LANDMARK EDITIONS, INC.

P.O. Box 270169 • 1402 Kansas Avenue • Kansas City, Missouri 64127
(816)241-4919

THE TIMEKEEPER

Written & Illustrated by

ANNA RIPHAHN

Dedicated to:
Jesus Christ,
who has blessed me
with his grace,
his mercy,
and his love.

COPYRIGHT © 1996 BY ANNA RIPHAHN

International Standard Book Number: 0-933849-62-1 (LIB.BDG.)

Library of Congress Cataloging-in-Publication Data
Riphahn, Anna, 1981-
    The timekeeper / written and illustrated by Anna Riphahn.
    p.   cm.
    Summary: When a mysterious stranger arrives in a chaotic land
without time, he separates nights from days and minutes from hours
only to find that people remain dissatisfied.
ISBN 0-933849-62-1 (lib.bdg. : alk. paper)
 1. Children's writings, American.
[1. Time—Fiction.
 2. Fantasy. 3. Children's writings. 4. Stories in rhyme.]

I. Title.
PZ8.3.R4813Ti   1996
[E]—dc20   96-12957
                                           CIP
                                           AC

Creative Coordinator: David Melton
Editorial Coordinator: Nancy R. Thatch
Production Assistant: Brian Hubbard

Printed in the United States of America

Landmark Editions, Inc.
P.O. Box 270169
1402 Kansas Avenue
Kansas City, Missouri 64127
(816) 241-4919

THE TIMEKEEPER

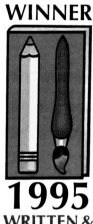

Anna Riphahn is a very persistent girl. She was determined to create a book that would win the National Written & Illustrated by... Awards Contest. When she entered her first book in the 1991 competition and won Third Place, she wasn't satisfied. So the next year, she created another book. When that book won Second Place, she still wasn't satisfied. Finally, in 1995 she wrote and illustrated a third book — THE TIMEKEEPER — and it won First Place!

But I have the feeling, if THE TIMEKEEPER had not won, Anna would have created a fourth book and even a fifth one, because her goal was to become the author and illustrator of a published book.

THE TIMEKEEPER was an extremely difficult book for Anna to compose and complete because it contains so many detailed illustrations. On every two-page spread, there is one major full-color illustration and three minor full-color illustrations, with two additional design elements in the arches of the borders above the text. All the individual borders on the outer edges of each and every page had to be designed and painted, too.

Anna also had to design and paint elaborate settings of landscapes, the village, and Mother Nature's gardens. She created detailed exteriors and interiors of buildings, too, and she drew and painted enough clocks to fill a pawnshop to overflowing. The story also included people, not one or two at a time, but standing in crowds, which required Anna to draw and paint enough people to fill the scenes. The project involved many hours of hard work and concentration. It was definitely an immense undertaking for a thirteen-year-old girl.

Because Anna and her parents live about an hour's drive from Kansas City, we saw them more often than we normally see other winners and their families. When Anna had questions or wanted our advice about her poetry or illustrations, the Riphahns would come to our offices for consultations. So Editor Nan Thatch and I had the privilege of witnessing in person the step-by-step evolvement of THE TIMEKEEPER. We enjoyed that experience, and we liked seeing Anna and her parents so often. They are very outgoing and personable people who possess and frequently unleash great senses of humor.

As you turn the pages of this extraordinary book, I am confident you will agree that Anna's time and efforts were well-spent. Her book is indeed an outstanding achievement!

Now, thanks to Anna's skills and imagination, you are about to enter a land without time and meet a man who will affect everyone's life with a wave of his hands and a tick of his clock. You are about to meet the Timekeeper and see the challenges he meets and the wonders he performs.

—David Melton
Creative Coordinator
Landmark Editions, Inc.

This story is written
In verse and in rhyme,
But cannot begin with —
"Once upon a time."

For it happened in a land
Before time was found,
Where the past and the future
Were nowhere around.

This place was quite strange,
For high in the air,
The sun never set, and
The moon remained there.

The sky always stayed
So light and so bright,
That no one could tell
The day from the night.

The roosters weren't sure
Just when they should crow,
And the owls never hooted
'Cause the sun was aglow.

The mice had to search
For food in the light,
Which pleased all the cats,
Who mewed with delight!

And the people, oh my!
They couldn't tell when
To sleep or to wake, or
When work should begin.

"QUIET!" yelled those who
Were trying to snooze.
The others yelled back,
"We'll do as we choose!"

Some people were early,
While others were late,
'Cause no one was sure of
The time or the date.

The people were disturbed
And filled with distress,
For this land without time
Was an absolute mess!

Then came the Timekeeper,
A stately old man.
Great powers had he
At his instant command.

With a wave of his hand,
He ordered the skies
To make the moon set and
Make the sun rise.

He brought forth a clock
That divided the hours
Into minutes and seconds.
Such were his powers.

The clock it did tick.
It tocked out the time
And announced every hour
By sounding its chime.

"What a marvelous clock!"
The people rejoiced.
"We want clocks of our own!"
They eagerly voiced.

And clocks soon appeared
On land and on seas,
In houses, on towers,
And even on trees.

When the sun at last set
And brought the dark night,
The moon rose on high
And cast its soft light.

Then all of the people
Went home to their beds.
They blew out their candles
And lay down their heads.

At dawn the next morning,
The sun spread its glow.
The roosters awakened
And started to crow.

And the people awoke
To greet the new day,
To breakfast and dress,
And be on their way.

All adults went to work
And children to class.
The clocks turned and chimed
To make the time pass.

The Timekeeper was pleased
At the order he'd brought.
Now the people were happy...
Or that's what he thought.

But...all were not happy.
The workers soon groaned,
"Our days are too long.
We're exhausted!" they moaned.

"No! No!" said their bosses.
"Days won't be reduced.
We need to add hours,
So more is produced."

"That's right!" said the farmers.
"We need time to plow.
So make the days longer,
Right here and right now!"

"STOP!" yelled the farmhands,
"Enough is enough!
To work longer days
Would really be tough!"

"We want short days, too,"
The schoolchildren pleaded.
"We're studying too much.
More playtime is needed!"

"We agree!" said their teachers.
"We need more vacations
From nouns and from verbs,
And from multiplications!"

Soon people assembled.
They marched in the street.
They yelled at the Timekeeper!
They stomped with their feet!

Their great show of anger
Made the Timekeeper worry.
And when he left town,
He left in a hurry!

He hoped Mother Nature
Could clear up the mess.
He sped to her doorstep;
He knew her address.

"Please help me!" he pleaded.
"Everyone's so uptight
With the length of the days
And the hours left at night.

"They're all very angry.
There's no one who's quiet.
If you cannot help me,
The people may riot!"

Mother Nature replied,
"I think we'd be wise
To settle their problems
With a compromise.

"To meet their demands and
All of their reasons,
I'll divide each year into
Four major seasons.

"To please all the bosses
And win farmers' praise,
In Spring and in Summer,
We'll make longer days.

"To calm all the workers
And stop all the fights,
In Fall and in Winter,
We'll lengthen the nights."

From the east to the west,
From the south to the north,
She unleashed her powers
And brought seasons forth.

The Timekeeper thanked her
For all her assistance.
His walk back to town was
Not a long distance.

The people were waiting
For him to return.
"What plan do you have?"
They wanted to learn.

He said, "Mother Nature
Has the time rearranged,
So the length of your days
By seasons are changed."

Then he told them of Winter,
Spring, Summer, and Fall.
They liked the new seasons
And agreed to them all.

"How can we thank you?"
They asked the old man.
He said, "Use your time
The best that you can.

"Work when you work,
But take time to play.
Make the most of each hour
By night and by day.

Once
upon
a
time...

"Be of good hope and
Be of good cheer.
Be kind to each other.
Be glad that you're here."

And, thanks to the Timekeeper,
His clock and its chime,
Their stories can start with —
"Once upon a time..."

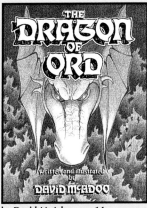

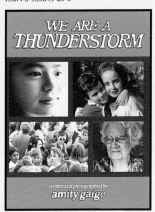

BY STUDENTS!®
ILLUSTRATED BY... AWARDS FOR STUDENTS –

WORLD WAR WON

by Dav Pilkey, age 19
Cleveland, Ohio

A thought-provoking parable! Two kings halt an arms race and learn to live in peace. This outstanding book launched Dav's professional career. He now has many books published.
Printed Full Color
ISBN 0-933849-22-2

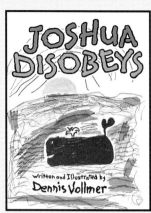

JOSHUA DISOBEYS

Written and Illustrated by Dennis Vollmer

by Dennis Vollmer, age 6
Grove Oklahoma

A baby whale's curiosity gets him into a lot of trouble. GUINNESS BOOK OF RECORDS lists Dennis as the youngest author/illustrator of a published book.
Printed Full Color
ISBN 0-933849-12-5

THE HALF & HALF DOG

written and illustrated by LISA GROSS

by Lisa Gross, age 12
Santa Fe, New Mexico

A touching story of self-esteem! A puppy is laughed at because of his unusual appearance. His search for acceptance is told with sensitivity and humor. Wonderful illustrations.
Printed Full Color
ISBN 0-933849-13-3

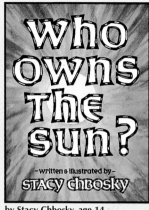

WHO OWNS THE SUN?

–written & illustrated by– STACY CHBOSKY

by Stacy Chbosky, age 14
Pittsburgh, Pennsylvania

A powerful plea for freedom! This emotion-packed story of a young slave touches an essential part of the human spirit. Made into a film by Disney Educational Productions.
Printed Full Color
ISBN 0-933849-14-1

OLIVER and the OIL SPILL

written and illustrated by ARUNA CHANDRASEKHAR

by Aruna Chandrasekhar, age 9
Houston, Texas

A touching and timely story! When the lives of many otters are threatened by a huge oil spill, a group of concerned people come to their rescue. Wonderful illustrations.
Printed Full Color
ISBN 0-933849-33-8

Life in the ghetto

written and illustrated by ANIKA D. THOMAS

by Anika D. Thomas, age 13
Pittsburgh, Pennsylvania

A compelling autobiography! A young girl's heartrending account of growing up in the tough inner-city neighborhood. The illustrations match the mood of this gripping story.
Printed Two Colors
ISBN 0-933849-34-6

A STONE PROMISE
BY CARA REICHEL

by Cara Reichel, age 15
Rome, Georgia

Elegant and eloquent! A young stonecutter vows to create a great statue for his impoverished village. But his fame almost stops him from fulfilling that promise.
Printed Two Colors
ISBN 0-933849-35-4

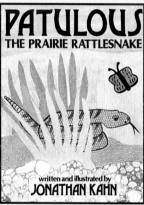

PATULOUS THE PRAIRIE RATTLESNAKE

written and illustrated by JONATHAN KAHN

by Jonathan Kahn, age 9
Richmond Heights, Ohio

A fascinating nature story! While Patulous, the prairie rattlesnake, searches for food, he must try to avoid the claws and fangs of his own enemies.
Printed Full Color
ISBN 0-933849-36-2

SPECIAL DAY

written & illustrated by DUBRAVKA KOLANOVIĆ

by Dubravka Kolanovic, age 18
Savannah, Georgia

A boy enjoys a wonderful day with his grandparents, a dog, a cat, and a playful bear that is always hungry. Clearly written, brilliantly illustrated — little kids love this book!
Printed Full Color
ISBN 0-933849-45-1

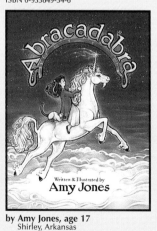

Abracadabra

Written & Illustrated by Amy Jones

by Amy Jones, age 17
Shirley, Arkansas

A whirlwind adventure! An enchanted unicorn helps a young girl rescue her eccentric aunt from the evil Sultan of Zabar. A charming story. Lovely illustrations add a magical glow!
Printed Full Color
ISBN 0-933849-46-X

THOMAS RACCOON'S FANTASTIC AIRSHOW

written & illustrated by SHINTARO MAEDA

by Shintaro Maeda, age 8
Wichita, Kansas

A terrific picture-story book! The birds won't fly in the airshow unless Mr. Eagle approves. Since everyone is afraid of Mr. Eagle, Thomas Raccoon must face the grumpy old bird alone.
Printed Full Color
ISBN 0-933849-51-6

THE SUNFLOWER

MILES MacGREGOR

by Miles MacGregor, age 12
Phoenix, Arizona

A beautifully illustrated legend! To save his people from starvation, an Indian boy must search for the seeds of a marvelous Sunflower that can light the sky and warm the earth.
Printed Full Color
ISBN 0-933849-52-4

Your Students Will Want To See All These Exciting Books!

Dav Pilkey
age 19

Dennis Vollmer
age 6

Lisa Gross
age 12

Stacy Chbosky
age 14

A. Chandrasekhar
age 9

Anika Thomas
age 13

Cara Reichel
age 15

Jonathan Kahn
age 9

D. Kolanovic
age 18

Amy Jones
age 17

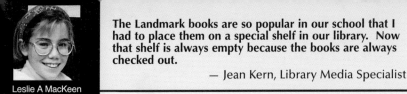

Leslie A MacKeen
age 9

Elizabeth Haidle
age 13

Heidi Salter
age 19

Lauren Peters
age 7

Jayna Miller
age 19

Alise Leggat
age 8

Lisa Butenhoff
age 13

Shintaro Maeda
age 8

Miles MacGregor
age 12

Kristin Pedersen
age 18

by Leslie Ann MacKeen, age 9
Winston-Salem, North Carolina
Loaded with fun and puns! When Jeremiah T. Fitz's car stops running, several animals offer suggestions for fixing it. The results are hilarious. The illustrations are charming.
Printed Full Color
ISBN 0-933849-19-2

by Elizabeth Haidle, age 13
Beaverton, Oregon
A very touching story! The grumpiest Elfkin learns to cherish the friendship of others after he helps an injured snail and befriends an orphaned boy. Absolutely beautiful.
Printed Full Color
ISBN 0-933849-20-6

by Heidi Salter, age 19
Berkeley, California
Spooky and wonderful! To save her vivid imagination, a young girl must confront the Great Grey Grimly himself. The narrative is filled with suspense. Vibrant illustrations.
Printed Full Color
ISBN 0-933849-21-4

by Lauren Peters, age 7
Kansas City, Missouri
The Christmas that almost wa When Santa Claus takes a vaca Mrs. Claus and the elves go strike. Toys aren't made. Coo aren't baked. Super illustrations
Printed Full Color
ISBN 0-933849-25-7

by Jayna Miller, age 19
Zanesville, Ohio
The funniest Halloween ever! When Jammer the Rabbit takes all the treats, his friends get even. Their hilarious scheme includes a haunted house and mounds of chocolate.
Printed Full Color
ISBN 0-933849-37-0

by Alise Leggat, age 8
Culpepper, Virginia
Amy J. Kendrick wants to play football, but her mother wants her to become a ballerina. Their clash of wills creates hilarious situations. Clever, delightful illustrations.
Printed Full Color
ISBN 0-933849-39-7

by Lisa Kirsten Butenhoff, age 13
Woodbury, Minnesota
The people of a Russian Village face the winter without warm clothes or enough food. Then their lives are improved by a young girl's gifts. A tender story with lovely illustrations.
Printed Full Color
ISBN 0-933849-40-0

by Jennifer Brady, age 17
Columbia, Missouri
When poachers capture a prid lions, a native boy tries to free animals. A skillfully told s Glowing illustrations illuminate African adventure.
Printed Full Color
ISBN 0-933849-41-9

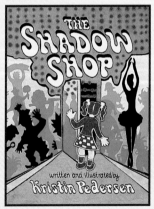

by Kristin Pedersen, age 18
Etobicoke, Ont., Canada
A mysterious parable, told in rhyme. When Thelma McMurty trades her shadow, she thinks she will live happily ever after. But an old gypsy knows better. The collage illustrations are brilliant!
Printed Full Color
ISBN 0-933849-53-2

by Laura Hughes, age 8
Woonsocket, Rhode Island
When a Dakota Indian girl finds a herd of buffalo, the big hunt of the year begins! An exciting fiction-based-on-fact story with wonderful illustrations that younger children will enjoy.
Printed Full Color
ISBN 0-933849-57-5

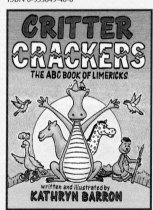

by Kathryn Barron, age 13
Emo, Ont., Canada
Funny from A to Z! Kathryn's hilarious limericks and delightfully witty illustrations provide laughs, page after page! An absolutely charming book for young children.
Printed Full Color
ISBN 0-933849-58-3

by Taramesha Maniatty, age 15
Morrisville, Vermont
A young man is determined tha dog-sledding team will win the race during the competition, he is forc make the most difficult decision c life. Brilliant text and paintings.
Printed Full Color
ISBN 0-933849-59-1

All BOOKS FOR STUDENTS BY STUDENTS® are 29 pages, printed on 100-pound, acid-free paper. They have laminated hardcovers and reinforced library bindings for added durability.